OUT OF THE MIRROR: A WORKBOOK OF HEALING FOR ADULT CHILDREN OF COVERT NARCISSISTS

BY: BETH MCDONALD, M.A., LPC

Contents

INTRODUCTION

Chances are that if you've picked up this workbook, you have a pretty good idea what a narcissist is. They can be self-centered, egotistical, self-absorbed, and see themselves as superior to everyone around them. If you have ever worked for a narcissist you know they will take the credit for your work, put you down to make themselves look better, take every opportunity to tell you how amazing they are, and if they're angry WATCH OUT. A narcissist's anger can tear the house down and take everyone with it. They will go after your most vulnerable insecurities, broadcast your secrets, and forget about arguing or defending yourself—a narcissist is a master at turning everything you say into a personal attack. Scott Peck (1983) called them "people of the lie" because they will surround themselves with lies in order to protect their fragile egos and remain above reproach. Arguments or even discussions become confusing because the narcissist can twist your words around to the point that you forgot what the heck it was you were trying to say in the first place. It's like a conversational spider web that you will do anything to get out of, even if it means admitting it was all your fault. In fact, by the time your narcissist boss is through with you, you might actually believe you were at fault and end up apologizing! They come out smelling like a rose and you slink back to your cubicle wondering what planet you were just on.

Working for a narcissist is bad enough, but you can always leave (once you've had some therapy) and find a new job. What if the narcissist isn't your boss, but your parent?

Growing up with a parent who is a narcissist causes children to doubt who they are, what they think, how they feel, what interests them, what they're good at, what they need, and with no sense of what real love looks or feels like. One of the significant hallmarks of Narcissistic Personality Disorder (NPD) is that people with the disorder lack empathy; they can't recognize the feelings experienced by another human being. The ability to empathize is what makes us compassionate, to have respect for another person's boundaries, to intuit what they need or put their needs above our own. Empathy is what drives human beings to give without receiving and to love unconditionally. A narcissistic parent is unable to do that; their needs come first, and they expect *their children* to give without receiving—to love them unconditionally. They don't see their children as separate individuals; they see them as reflections of their own image, like mirrors. If little Johnny does well in school, it reflects positively on mom and dad; but if little Johnny struggles, he makes mom and dad look like bad parents. And he's doing it on purpose! Not only is Johnny failing, but he's lazy or rebellious, and manipulative. Children of narcissists learn very quickly to hide their true selves and numb their own feelings, and at the same develop an acute awareness of the needs and expectations of others.

Types of Narcissists: Overt and Covert

There are two types of narcissists: the overt narcissist and the covert narcissist. The overt type is very grandiose, arrogant, bold, bossy, preoccupied with success, exploitive, entitled, and require constant attention and praise. They can also be overtly abusive: drug users, physically or sexually abusive, criminals, mentally ill, or neglectful—but not always and not to everyone. Think of someone like Bing Crosby who was a popular singer in the 1950's. After he died his four sons talked about how abusive he was to them when they were growing up. His son Gary wrote that his dad would come home at 6:00 pm and by 6:05 pm would have Gary "bent over and my pants taken down and beat till I bled. He was never an enraged, insane man. He was very methodical." Bing Crosby was seen by the world as a great family man, a great husband and the pinnacle of success, but he had many, many secrets. Like all narcissists, he presented an image of himself that was above reproach, only it was all lies (Haller, 1983). Overt narcissists are not playing—they will stop at nothing to get what they want, and are quite frankly admired for how successful they are at getting it. Now, behind the scenes their personal lives are a disaster, but on the outside it's all shiny and pretty.

Covert narcissists, on the other hand, *want* all those things, and truly believe they deserve them, but appear to others as modest, humble, giving, and even shy. It is those closest to them, probably only their families, who see them as they truly are: angry, critical, blaming, depressed, demeaning, scapegoating, defensive and moody. They do have the ability to be kind and giving, but there's an anger that's always beneath the surface, and seems to come out of nowhere for no apparent reason. The conflict for covert narcissists is that they aren't able to attain the level success and admiration that, in their minds, they so richly deserve. Like the overt narcissist, any hint of failure is never their fault; they'll blame anyone but themselves, usually their spouse and children. Covert narcissists can become extremely verbally abusive, but for the most part, that's where the obvious abuse ends. This type of narcissism is more of a mind game, and people who grow up in households where one or both parents were covert narcissists enter adulthood sort of shaking their heads. They know something wasn't right, but for the life of them they can't figure out what it was—and neither can anyone else. For goodness sakes, they had everything! What's there to complain about?

Codependency

Covertly narcissistic family system are the most difficult to detect, and very little is known about them. Often, adult children of narcissistic parents have symptoms similar to adult children of alcoholics (ACOA), without any history abuse in their family of origin. In covertly narcissistic families, everything seems fine, there was nothing overtly wrong, and from the outside seemed completely normal. People report that they had a good childhood, were well taken care of, involved in scouts, played on little league teams, graduated from high school, went on to college, and so on. Neither mom nor dad drank or took drugs, no one was being beaten or spent time in jail, so where do these codependent behaviors come from? The problem, and the source of tremendous emotional wounding for adult children raised in covertly narcissistic homes, is that the children had to meet their parents' needs and never were allowed to need anything. These are families where the kids have more than enough, so how can they be unhappy? Are they just selfish or whiny? No, they aren't. To survive their families, they learned to not trust people, never ask for anything, and to empathize with others instead of themselves. Often adult children of narcissists become teachers, nurses, therapists, ministers and other helping professionals. They are highly intuitive, compassionate, bright and giving. The problem is that they don't expect much in return and end up in one-sided relationships and dysfunctional work places that take without ever giving back. The unspoken promise made to children of narcissists was that if they give what their parents what they want, and be what their parents want them to be, they will finally be good enough to be cared about. Of course, that didn't work as children, and it doesn't work when they're adults, but that pattern of behavior is deeply entrenched in the personality. It is a dysfunctional pattern of caring for others in order to be cared for that is called codependency.

About the Workbook

This workbook was designed specifically for *adult children of covert narcissistic parents. I will help you identify and understand covertly narcissistic parenting, some of the family dynamics you grew up in, how it may have affected you as a child, and to learn to have empathy for the amazing little kid you were who managed to survive. We will look at some of the behaviors of codependency and of adult children of narcissists, as well as go on a journey of discovering who you are as an individual. What are some of your unique qualities? What do you love? What are your dreams? What are your strengths and weaknesses? Finally, through a series of exercises, we will tackle things you might want to change in your life. Even little changes can make a huge difference; they don't have to be monumental (although lets no rule that out)!

This is a beginning. Go at your own pace, gather some of your friends or do it alone, talk about it, or keep it private. Some of what you learn may be painful, but the truth really will set you free.

The term "adult children" essentially means that the survival skills learned in childhood to cope in a dysfunctional family system are still being employed in adulthood. For example: If adult children make a mistake at work, they might lie about it when the mistake wasn't intentional, it wasn't a big deal and it would've been perfectly fine to admit to. An adult child doesn't know this, doesn't think about it, and will lie when telling the truth would've been just as easy.

"The experience of one's own truth, and the postambivalent
knowledge of it, makes it possible to return to one's own world
of feelings at an adult level—without paradise,
but with the ability to mourn."

----*Alice Miller, The Drama of the Gifted Child*

PART I: THE PAST

Chapter One

Understanding the Covertly Narcissistic Parent

What do children need in order to grow up and lead healthy lives? Lives where they are able to love and be loved, use their gifts and talents in jobs they find satisfying, and be involved in their communities? Alfred Adler said that children learn to have courage to meet the challenges of life when they've received a solid foundation of respect, support, encouragement and love from their parents. This doesn't mean that in order to be happy as an adult you needed to have had perfect parents, far from it. Everyone's parents have flaws, personal problems and issues. What healthy parents do have, is the ability to see their children as individuals with their own emotions, feelings, thoughts, ideas, talents, dreams, strengths, weaknesses and personalities. These parents get their own emotional needs met by their peers and are able to differentiate their worth as a person from the performance of their children. They expect their children to make mistakes and don't see them *as* their mistakes. They speak to their children with respect, not contempt. They allow their children to experience natural consequences of their behavior and set reasonable boundaries for them. Healthy parents create households of cooperation and mutual respect where children feel needed and important. Not *more* important than anyone else or *more* needed than others, but *as* important and *as* needed. A healthy family is a respectful one where people are allowed to be individuals. Just because dad never got to fulfill his dreams of being a professional baseball player doesn't mean Jr. has to play little league softball if he doesn't like softball. Maybe Jr. likes ballet or piano and could care less about sports.

Children that grow up in healthy homes feel *as good* as others. Not better, not worse, but equal to. As adults they face the same life storms that are inevitable, but feel capable of dealing with whatever comes up and have courage and self-confidence. Failures don't define them and aren't confirmation of their worthlessness; failures are seen as mistakes or lessons, and can be overcome in time.

Covertly narcissistic families are quite the opposite. From the outside looking in, everything looks great. If you didn't live in the house you might assume it's the healthy family I described. Dad isn't drunk in the front yard wearing a bathrobe howling at the moon and mom isn't being arrested for shoplifting at the grocery store. That would be obvious and everyone would feel sorry for the poor kids living in those conditions. In a covertly narcissistic family dad goes to work every day, mows the lawn on Saturdays, maybe plays a little golf here and there and provides a decent living for his family. Mom might work or be a stay at home mom, but she takes good care of the children and has a clean home; nothing flashy, just a normal middle or upper-middle class family. What does happen behind closed doors is definitely not normal. Covertly narcissistic parents (which can either be mom, dad, or both) expect their children to meet their emotional needs, and don't see them as separate, unique individuals; they are seen as extensions or mirror images of themselves—of *who they think they should be.* Children of covert narcissists don't get to have feelings or emotions because they don't matter. All that matters is what the parents need in order to feel better than anyone else, to be admired and envied, and to project an image of perfection to the world.

Covert Narcissism

There is a very distinct difference between the behavior of overt and covert narcissists, but it's very, very subtle. The root issues are the same, the motivation is the same, but they don't act the same way. In order to understand covert narcissism and how it has affected your life, it's so important to understand what drives them both. Think of covert narcissism as a closeted or cloaked version of overt narcissism.

The Diagnostic and Statistical Manual-5 (DSM-5, 2013) lists a series of criteria that a person must meet in order to be diagnosed with NPD by a mental health professional. The DSM-5 describes NPD as: *A pervasive pattern of grandiosity (in fantasy or behavior), need for admiration, and lack of empathy, beginning in early childhood and present in a variety of contexts, as indicated by five (or more) of the following:*

1. Has a grandiose sense of self-importance (e.g., exaggerates achievements and talents, expects to be recognized as superior without commensurate with achievements).

2. Is preoccupied with fantasies of unlimited success, power, brilliance, beauty, or ideal love.

3. Believes that he or she is "special" and unique and can only be understood by, or should associate with, other special or high-status people (or institutions).

4. Requires excessive admiration.

5. Has a sense of entitlement (i.e., unreasonable expectations of especially favorable treatment or automatic compliance with his or her expectations).

6. Is interpersonally exploitative (i.e., takes advantage of others to achieve his or her own ends).

7. Lacks empathy; is unwilling to recognize or identify with the feelings and needs of others.

8. Shows arrogant, haughty behaviors or attitudes (pp. 669-670).

What makes these traits a personality disorder and not just annoying characteristics? The American Psychological Association (APA; 2013) states that people with personality disorders have: *pervasive, inflexible, and rigid patterns of thinking, feeling, behaving, or social interaction, which are associated with distress or impaired functioning in interpersonal or professional domains.* In other words, this is how they live, it's not just a knee jerk reaction to stress or chaos; it is a way that people with NPD see themselves and the world around them. It's important to note that no one chooses to be this way; people with NPD were raised in homes where they weren't nurtured appropriately and can't give what they don't have. NPD is difficult to treat; in part because there is so much confusion about diagnosing the disorder among clinicians and the assessments that exist are self-reported (Dickinson & Pincus, 2003). Not only that, but narcissists don't typically seek counseling because they really believe their problems are caused by everyone around them. They send their spouses and children to counseling instead. In fact, overt narcissists are blissfully unaware and unconcerned with how their behavior affects the people in their lives. They remain unconflicted about who they are and what they appear to be: they believe they are superior and they act like they believe they are superior, they believe they are entitled and they act like they are entitled, they believe they should get all the attention and they act like they should get all the attention. And you know what? They usually are quite successful, and even if they aren't, they believe they are! If they do experience anything that might resemble failure, they are not to blame; others are (Dickinson & Pincus, 1994).

Conversely, covert narcissists feel a great deal of conflict around what they think they deserve and how they appear. Whereas overt narcissists appear to be conceited ego-maniacs, covert narcissists appear to be hypersensitive, anxious, timid and insecure. If you met them at a party or church you might think they were shy and modest people, quite humble, even self-deprecating. They certainly would not be the person with a big crowd around them telling stories and needing to be the center of attention, but they wish they were. Covert narcissists have the same grandiose fantasies of overt narcissists, but only those close to them ever see that side of their personalities (Wink, 1992).

What is it like, day to day, for children to be raised in a narcissistic family? Everything they do is a reflection of their parents. Think about what that means. When a narcissist looks at their children, they see themselves. They don't see a person separate from themselves, they see their own reflection, as though they are looking in a mirror. Miller (1983) called the children of narcissists "echoes" because whatever they do, think, or feel belongs to the parent, *is* the parent. If a child is successful at anything, preferably something important to the parents, that success is reflected back as belonging to the narcissist. What it says to mom or dad is the child cares enough about them to be successful. Now, if the child is not successful, for whatever reason, that failure is also reflected back as belonging to the narcissist. For the narcissist, love equals performance and performance equals love. Their thought process is: "If you love me you will make me look good, and when I look good, I will love you." Unfortunately, the expectations of narcissistic parents change constantly— what pleased them yesterday may or may not please them today. Children have to try and figure out what they can do, or what they didn't do, to earn their parents' approval. When they do fail to please, they almost always interpret this as a sign of their own worthlessness, and for good reason: the narcissist blames them.

Let's use the example of sports to illustrate how this dynamic might work. There is no better place to see narcissistic parent-child relations than on the field during a youth sporting event (and in the car ride home). Maybe dad is the coach of his daughter's soccer team and he always wanted to be good at sports when he was a kid, but never got the chance or just wasn't very good. It's very important to him to win, to impress the other adults and the other coaches; not only by coaching a winning team, but by having a daughter who excels as well. It's not about teaching the girls sportsmanship or teamwork, it's not about having fun and getting exercise, and it may not even be about his daughter ever wanting to play soccer in the first place. It is about a grown man trying to be what he never was through his daughter. If she does well and he has the best player on the team, it not only makes him look like a winner to the other parents, but it shows him that his daughter loves him enough to work hard and play well. If you think in terms of her being a reflection of him running around out there, it's not his daughter he sees, it's himself, trying to get what he never could as a child—what he was entitled to then, and what he is entitled to now. He might take her out for ice cream after the game and tell her how proud he is of her, which is great, that's what a good dad would do. But, what if she isn't a good soccer player or didn't do well during the game? A covert narcissist dad/coach isn't going to flip out and start yelling at little Suzie right on the field in front of everyone; he's going to wait until they get in the car. The anger of a narcissist seems to come out of nowhere and can be like a tornado, destroying everything in its path. Children as young as six will be called "lazy" or "incompetent" and worse by a parent who ten minutes ago was telling them: "It's alright, everyone has bad days, better luck next time, and you tried your best." That angry father may not speak to them for days after a loss on the field. Narcissistic parents will appear to care about the performance of their children and do all the things they're supposed to do to support them, but underneath all of that caring is a very selfish motive: themselves.

This anger isn't always expressed, sometimes it's more passive-aggressive and will show up later, or come out in a way that might seem like a joke or teasing, but is actually sort of mean. Covert narcissists can wait for weeks to share their displeasure. Dad might make a joke about his daughter's poor soccer performance at a family birthday party or make some snide remark in front of her friends when she's talking about how much fun she had a soccer practice. Jokes and teasing can feel "biting" because it isn't funny, it's mean. Teasing is a very subtle way that covert narcissists express true anger, but it catches people off guard. Sort of "haha/ouch" is the feeling you can get when humor is used as a weapon.

Narcissistic Parents

NPD is very difficult for clinicians to assess because narcissists want to appear perfect; they will very seldom admit to having grandiose fantasies of superiority. Covert narcissists don't see themselves as having these feelings in the first place! The most commonly used assessment consists of forty questions and is called the Narcissistic Personality Inventory (NPI-40; Raskin & Hall, 1979, 1981). A shorter version was developed that has sixteen questions (NPI-16; Ames, Anderson & Rose, 2006) and is useful when asking questions to assess NPD in a parent or caregiver. The revised NPI-16 (McDonald, 2013) is designed to address behaviors of a narcissistic parent from the viewpoint of an adult child. Because covert narcissists do share the same characteristics as overt narcissists, and these are most often only seen by those closest to them, it is appropriate to use the NPI-16-(Revised) to assess the parents as well. The goal of using this questionnaire is to help you put a name to what you felt as a child and to help you become aware, maybe for the first time, of how difficult it was to grow up in a narcissistic family. If the results of the questionnaire don't indicate that your mother or father (or both) were narcissists, but you still feel that some of these behaviors help you to understand them, then it's beneficial.

A note about assessments: they are wonderful tools, but they aren't crystal balls. They are really designed to bring issues to light, indicate where a person may be struggling, and rule out other symptoms or root causes that may be influencing a current situation. They may raise more questions than they answer, and that's great! The assessments, questionnaires, and exercises in this workbook are meant to be done in progression, so that a picture not only begins to emerge about how your family operated, but open up the possibilities for who you can become.

NPI-16 Informant Report (Revised)

This questionnaire is from your perspective now as an adult. Please check the answer that most closely describes your parent or caregiver that is the subject of the assessment:

My parent(s):

1.	a) _____ believes they can do things better than anyone else.
	b) _____ believes they can do some things well, but others do things as well or better.
2.	a) _____ gets mad when they are not the center of attention.
	b) _____ allows others to be the center of attention.
3.	a) _____ thinks they are special.
	b) _____ feels they are no worse or better than anyone else.
4.	a) _____ likes to have authority over others.
	b) _____ lets others lead.
5.	a) _____ always want their own way and can be manipulative to get it.
	b) _____ don't need to have things their own way and don't like being manipulative.
6.	a) _____ insist on being respected, even when that respect is undeserved.
	b) _____ are willing to earn respect and gives others respect when due.
7.	a) _____ is a show off (brag about their accomplishments, etc.)
	b) _____ try not to show off (don't brag about accomplishments, etc.)
8.	a) _____ act like they know what they're doing, even when they don't.
	b) _____ are sometimes unsure about what they're doing.
9.	a) _____ thinks everyone wants to hear their stories.
	b) _____ can sometimes tell a good story and enjoy listening to other people's stories.

| 10. | a) _____ expect others to be perfect. |
| | b) _____ know and accept that other people are not perfect. |

| 11. | a) _____ really like being the center of attention. |
| | b) _____ don't really need to be the center of attention. |

| 12. | a) _____ hates to be criticized, but are very critical of others. |
| | b) _____ don't mind constructive criticism and is not critical of others. |

| 13. | a) _____ wanted to be a great person that other people admired. |
| | b) _____ wanted to be a good person that people loved. |

| 14. | a) _____ don't like to hear other people's ideas or thoughts. |
| | b) _____ don't mind having other people share their ideas or thoughts. |

| 15. | a) _____ always think they can could do things better than everyone else. |
| | b) _____ feel that they are capable of doing things well, but so are others. |

| 16. | a) _____ think they're special. |
| | b) _____ never think of themselves as special. |

Totals: _____ (a) _____ (b)

If you answered more questions with (a) than you did (b) then your parent(s) may have/had

narcissistic traits. If you have significantly higher (a) answers than (b) answers (over 50%), then your

parent(s) could possibly be diagnosed as having NPD. Remember, the tools and assessments we will

be using are not meant to figure out your parents, they are designed to help you to become more

aware of parent-child relationship dynamics that were going on in the home you grew up in.

** A note about the reflection questions and writing that follow these questionnaires and assessments. I am a huge
believer in the power of journaling, and when we write by hand, our words are more connected to our hearts. Writing*

helps you internalize information, remember it, and connect to it. I encourage you to write freely and whatever comes to mind, don't over-think it!

Write down any thoughts you have or memories that came to mind as a result of answering this questionnaire:

_____

_____

_____

_____

Reflections (about anything):

_____

_____

_____

_____

_____

_____

_____

"Life can only be understood backwards; but it must be lived forwards."

— *Søren Kierkegaard*

"True love heals and affects spiritual growth. If we do not grow because of someone else's love, it's generally because it is a counterfeit form of love."

— *John Bradshaw, Healing the Shame that Binds You*

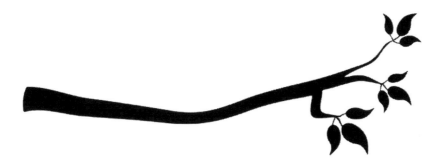

Chapter 2

Understanding Family Dynamics

In order to understand your current thoughts and behaviors—to become aware of *why* you do what you do, it's important to examine and explore the narcissistic family system. Some people feel uncomfortable at this stage of the process because they don't want to place blame on their parents. What is all too easy, however, is to put blame on themselves for everything. Healing is never about blame—healing is about truth. Children who are raised in covertly narcissistic families learn to hide their feelings and mask their true emotions very early on. What happens when children begin to assert themselves in a house where their needs and feelings are not only unimportant, and actually makes their parents angry? They learn, and become very good at, picking up on other people's feelings and moods. They can tell what mood their parents are in by the way they shut the front door or how their footsteps sound. With one look they can intuit what is being required of them and try their hardest to meet their parents' expectations (or rebel, it can go either way). It doesn't always work, because those expectations change every day and are unspoken, but sometimes they manage to be "good" and this cycle of people pleasing is reinforced. Children with covertly narcissistic parents learn to not tell the truth, and they learn to lie—very, very well. They have no one to go to for guidance when they make a mistake or are afraid so they figure out how to cover up and present the image that their parents (and other authority figures) want to see. These children are incredibly lonely. Sure, they have everything, but that is not what children need. Alice Miller (1981) writes:

> *I sometimes ask myself whether it will ever be possible to full grasp the extent of the loneliness and desertion to which we were exposed to as children. Here I do not mean to speak, primarily, of children who were obviously uncared for or totally neglected, and who were always aware of this or at least grew up with knowledge that is was so. Apart from these extreme cases, there are large numbers of people who enter therapy in the belief (with which they grew up) that their childhood was happy and protected. (pp. 4-5)*

We're going to look now at some of the behaviors of covertly narcissistic parents from the viewpoint of the child. The NPI-16 was revised further (McDonald, 2013) as an assessment of early childhood to help you develop an awareness of yourself as a child rather than just looking at these behaviors from an adult perspective. Something to keep in mind is that in a household with siblings, there may be only one child who is the focus of narcissistic rage. In many cases it's the first born, or it may be the child who is the first born *and* same sex as the narcissistic parent. I've been writing *parents* in the plural for the sake of simplicity, but normally only one parent is narcissistic although that is not true in all cases. You may have brothers and sisters who have no idea what you're talking about when you bring up the subject of mom or dad being a covert narcissist, but that doesn't mean you're wrong. Siblings enjoy a certain freedom when one child has accepted the role of the narcissist pleaser; in fact, they often become the kind, nurturing parent to their siblings. Often children are even pitted against one another, and these relationships can remain broken into adulthood. As you begin to heal, remember that you all grew up in a very dysfunctional family; each child had to develop their own coping skills to survive it, and may have very different takes on what really happened at home.

A very important step for individuals, who are in recovery of any kind, is to learn to have compassion and to empathize with themselves as children. People forget how small and fragile an eight year old is, especially when they've felt like adults all their lives. It's true, most adult children of narcissists were expected to be miniature adults and never got to experience childhood. They grow up to be very, very hard on themselves. They still strive to be perfect and, and of course can't, so they always feel like failures, and have a harsh inner dialogue going on that would rival General Patton's. John Bradshaw (1990) said that the wounded inner child of the past is the source for human misery. The good news is that we can heal that inner child by seeing life through his or her eyes, and by learning to love them in spite of their so-called flaws.

NPI-16 Early Childhood Assessment (Revised)

This assessment is to help you understand your family system from your viewpoint as a child. Please check the answer that most closely describes your parent(s) or caregiver that is the subject of the assessment:

My parent(s):

1.	a) _____ took the credit for my success.
	b) _____ was proud of me if I did something well.
2.	a) _____ took my failures and mistakes personally.
	b) _____ helped me learn from my mistakes and failures.
3.	a) _____ wanted to associate with "high status" people.
	b) _____ felt that they were no worse and no better than other people.

4.	a) _____ demanded that I trusted them and respected them.
	b) _____ were trustworthy and respectful of me.
5.	a) _____ was a "know-it-all."
	b) _____ didn't always have to be right.
6.	a) _____ wanted constant praise and recognition for what they did for me.
	b) _____ didn't expect recognition and praise for what they did for me.
7.	a) _____ expected me to be perfect.
	b) _____ didn't expect me to be perfect.
8.	a) _____ was mean when no one was around (critical, sarcastic, demeaning, etc.)
	b) _____ was never intentionally mean.
9.	a) _____ gossiped about other family members
	b) _____ didn't gossip about people
10.	a) _____ was not warm, nurturing, or sympathetic.
	b) _____ was warm, nurturing, and sympathetic.
11.	a) _____ did not have many close friends.
	b) _____ had several very close friends.
12.	a) _____ expected me to meet their needs.
	b) _____ met their own needs and met mine too.
13.	a) _____ blamed other people for all of their problems.
	b) _____ took responsibility for their own problems.

14.	a) _____ were always comparing themselves to other people.
	b) _____ never compared themselves to other people.
15.	a) _____ gave love that was conditional.
	b) _____ loved me unconditionally.
16.	a) _____ would go into a rage for no reason.
	b) _____ was emotionally stable.

Totals: _____ (a) _____ (b)

If you answered more questions with (a) than you did (b) you may have grown up in a narcissistic family. You can also answer this questionnaire for both of your parents or other significant care-givers you had as a child. It would be interesting to notice if one parent differed significantly from the other in how you experienced their behavior towards you.

Write down any thoughts you have or memories that came to mind as a result of answering this questionnaire:

_____

_____

_____

_____

_____

_____

_____

"I am no bird; and no net ensnares me: I am a free human being with an independent will."
— Charlotte Brontë, Jane Eyre

"I'm not sure if resilience is ever achieved alone. Experience allows us to learn from example. But if we have someone who loves us—I don't mean who indulges us, but who loves us enough to be on our side—then it's easier to grow resilience, to grow belief in self, to grow self-esteem. And it's self-esteem that allows a person to stand up."

— *Maya Angelou*

Chapter 3

Understanding Childhood

Pressman & Pressman (1994) talk about the unspoken rules in a covertly narcissistic household, and the rules about communication are the most subtle and damaging. They insulate the parents from having to meet the needs of their children in such an underhanded way, that unless you were Freud Jr. you would never know what hit you. Not only does the communication style in a narcissistic family keep the parents from taking any responsibility for meeting their own needs or emotions, but it puts that responsibility squarely on the children. Three of the most common ways this happens is through passive-aggressive communication, triangulation, and lack of parental accessibility. These dysfunctional forms of communicating in the narcissistic family help to insulate the parents from dealing with their own feelings, and discourage the children from expressing theirs as well. When M. Scott Peck (1993) called narcissists "people of the lie," what he was referring to was this subtle, but effective process of insulating themselves from seeing or hearing the truth.

Passive Aggressive Communication

Alfred Adler (n.d.) wrote that in order to raise healthy children, parents should develop a relationship based on enjoyment, mutual respect, love and affection, mutual confidence and trust, and a feeling of belonging. Instead of talking to nag, scold, preach, and correct, parents should utilize talking to maintain a friendly relationship. He said that parents should speak to their children with the same respect and consideration that they would express to a good friend.

For example, in a healthy household, mom might ask one of the kids to take out the garbage and it would sound like this: "Hey Tim, before dinner would you mind taking out the garbage for me?" A covertly narcissistic mom might ask her son to take out the garbage like this: "I come home from work, exhausted, and as usual this house is a pigsty. Do I have to do everything around here myself? Did it even occur to you to take the garbage out? I suppose you have homework you haven't done either." Now, notice the difference. In the first example, mom is asking for what she needs and it isn't about her, how hard she works or how much better than everyone she is. It is about needing Tim to take out the garbage. Period. This discussion is about the garbage, and the fact that it needs to get out of the house and into the garbage bin outside. Would Tim please do that and thank you. In the second example, this indirect form of passive-aggressive communication is a spider web that Tim will find himself in and not know how to get out of. It is simultaneously shaming, blaming, humiliating and self-congratulating. Passive-aggressive communication is actually very hostile, there is so much anger seething around in it, but it's indirect—sort of like having someone punch you in the back and running away.

I'm going to break this conversation down so you can see how subtle, but destructive a communication style passive-aggressiveness really is. In order to elevate herself, mom has to subtly put down Tim: "I work hard, you don't do anything." Then, suddenly, the topic is Tim's lack of caring: "Did it even occur to you...?" This is the old one-two punch. This one-sided conversation quickly heads to Tim not doing his homework: "I suppose you didn't to your homework." Is this to imply that Tim never does his homework? What?! This whole exchange can last a total of 2 seconds, but you can imagine Tim is wondering what in the heck just happened here.

Indirect, passive-aggressive communication can also involve other people. Often people who employ this style of expressing themselves might "circle the wagons," meaning bring in other people to support their position and agree with them. After finishing with Tim, mom heads to the phone and starts telling one of her friends about Tim not taking out the garbage. She might be overheard saying she has a lazy son who doesn't appreciate her, and maybe she should take his phone away or ground him. Show some tough love. This makes mom feel like a good parent who is raising a son to be responsible, and her friends will probably agree with her! It sounds reasonable.

Let's keep analyzing the dynamics of this situation. What is mom communicating here? She goes to work and her work is exhausting, which she does for the good of the family, and everyone should be grateful. Look how hard mom works. Not only does she do everything in the house, but everyone else does nothing. If Tim was a good son, he would have looked around the house before his exhausted mother came home and noticed that the garbage should be taken out and probably cleaned up the rest of the house while he was at it. Not only that, but once again, Tim didn't do his homework because he's been sitting around doing nothing while mom does everything. The garbage has now become a symbol of appreciation, caring, responsibility, and worthiness, and school performance. What mom didn't know, and couldn't have known (because she didn't ask) is that Tim's homework was all done, he got an award at school, did some laundry and helped a little old lady across the street. All of which he didn't tell her because he already knows it wouldn't matter; not to mention she's already taken out the garbage in her high heels and is in the driveway telling her neighbor what a lazy son she has.

What subtle messages is Tim getting during this one-sided conversation?

_____

_____

_____

_____

How do you think it made Time feel to have his mom come home and talk to him like this?

_____

_____

_____

_____

What are some ways Tim might try to avoid getting yelled at by mom when she comes home from work the next time?

_____

_____

_____

_____

Circle words you think describe the feelings Tim might have when his mom talks to him like this:

Anxious   Trusting   Angry   Nervous   Secure   Sad

Excited   Secretive   Loved   Afraid   Confused

Avoidant   Respected   Ashamed   Happy   Lonely

Triangulation

When you're upset with someone or want to ask them a question, the healthiest and most effective way to do that is to go talk to them. This is not the way narcissistic parents communicate. Instead, they will either speak to someone through a third person, say for instance, another family member (even a pet), or talk to one family member about another. Think of a triangle instead of a straight line and you basically have the triangulating dynamic. Again, this takes the responsibility away from the narcissist and lays it at the feet of whoever they are talking about, or the third party who has unwittingly agreed to be used as a go-between. Let's say mom is still mad at Tim about the garbage, and at the dinner table is being very quiet, maybe acting a little pouty. Dad asks her what's wrong and she sighs and says "nothing," but gives Tim a look. Now everyone knows it has something to do with Tim, so dad asks if anything happened between them that she's upset about. "Well, I'm just so sick of coming home after a very stressful day at work, and nothing is done around here. I ended up having to take the garbage out myself while Tim sat on the couch and watched me do it. You're too easy on these kids. Oh never mind, what's the use? You let them do anything they want, so I'm always the bad guy." See how this conversation is in a circle? First of all, it is not a conversation to have at the dinner table in front of other siblings, it isn't about the garbage at all, and now the dad and the others kids are to blame as well! In covertly narcissistic families, triangulating pulls in a 3rd person who either does nothing (not OK) or has to get in the middle somehow. It's uncomfortable, to say the least, for everyone EXCEPT the narcissist, who could not be happier.

Another form of triangulating is, for all intents and purposes, gossiping. It isn't just for the sake of gossiping though, it's a way of roping in a third person to use as a "messenger" under the guise of "let's you and I be close and talk about so and so." I'll continue to use poor Tim as my example (sorry Tim). After dinner Mom is still mad at Tim, or hasn't gotten the attention, praise or sympathy she was looking for. Instead of going directly to Tim and telling him she's sorry, she was just tired and crabby and didn't mean to take it out on him, she goes into his sister's room and starts to tell her all about it. She maybe even cries a bit and talks about how everything she does is for the good of the family, but no one seems to care what she needs. This form of communication serves two purposes: 1) it is very martyr-y. Feel sorry for me, I am under-appreciated, and 2) go a talk to so and so and convince them to do what I want. What mom hopes is that the sister will go talk to Tim (and maybe dad too) and tell him to try harder because mom works so hard and to just be nice to her. She may even tell the sister things about Tim that he would be embarrassed to have anyone know. Triangulating often involves some major boundary crossing. This is very typical for a covertly narcissistic family because it doesn't remotely seem abusive or cruel, but you can see how convoluted it is. What triangulating does is divide and conquer the other members of the family and keep the attention on the narcissist. Mom didn't ask Tim about his day, she didn't ask his sister about her day, and more than likely did not ask dad about his day either. By 7:30 p.m. she might be in her room with a glass of Chardonnay and a cold compress. It is all about her.

Write down any triangulating conversations you remember from your childhood:

_____

_____

_____

_____

_____

_____

_____

Write the feelings you associate with this conversation:

_____

_____

_____

_____

If you could have changed this conversation in any way, what would have been different?

_____

_____

_____

_____

_____

From the example given above, what do you think your feelings would have been if this is the way your family actually communicated?

_____

_____

_____

Emotionally Inaccessible Parents

What is emotional accessibility? Emotionally accessible people let you know who they are and are truly interested in getting to know you, too. It is that simple. They are open, honest, transparent, vulnerable and genuine. A conversation with an emotionally accessible person is liberating; you feel good and probably better than you did before the conversation started, even when it may have been a difficult talk to have. It's equal and you feel safe. This will look a little different between two adults than it does between a parent and child, but the principle is the same. In covertly narcissistic families, conversations are one-sided, and children learn very quickly that going to their parents to share feelings will quickly turn into an advice giving session (you should've done this, you shouldn't have done that, I told you so, etc.) or that the parents are too busy to talk anyway. Conversations with covert narcissists are like mine fields and children never know what might set them off. Even benign subjects can trigger covert narcissists to begin a lecture that ends in blaming their children for a myriad of short-comings and/or character flaws. It's never about sharing, covert narcissists don't really listen, and conversations with them are like being trapped in a fun-house mirror at the fair—all the images are distorted versions of the true self, but all they seem real. Adults have difficulty dissecting the spider-web conversations they may find themselves in with narcissists, although they instinctively know something is "off." Children, however, interpret these images as true reflections of who they are without questioning their validity.

We're going to give our little Timmy a break and use another example to illustrate a typical conversation with an emotionally inaccessible (covert narcissist) parent. Sally is in tenth grade and really struggling with math. It makes no sense to her, she has asked the teacher for help and still doesn't get it; she has stayed after school for extra credit, and she still isn't passing. Her dad has taken away her phone, grounded her, and said if she can't get her grade to a B he won't let her to go to camp (where she will be a counselor for the first time). Sally tries to talk with her dad about how frustrated she is and how stupid she feels about not being able to improve her grade and asks him to help her. Dad's response is: "You never apply yourself, you just think you can talk on the phone with your friends and hang out all weekend and magically get your math grade up. Life does not work that way. You're going to stay every day after school and get off your lazy butt and do the work for a change, I'm so sick of hearing how "hard" things are for you, maybe if you didn't stuff your face with cookies all day you'd have more time for homework." What dad neglected to tell Sally, was that he had failed almost every math class he had ever taken, and spent most of his time in high school smoking pot and hanging out with his friends. He's also 50 pounds overweight. He also never graduated from high school. Do you think Sally will ask her Dad for help with math again?

An emotionally accessible parent would have been able to empathize with his daughter and share that he too struggled with math, that he knew how hard it could be and that he could see how hard Sally was trying. Dad might have offered to go talk to the math teacher or research some tutoring options for her. He didn't have to share any information about failing math or smoking pot, that wouldn't help her or be appropriate, he just needed to have the emotional maturity to "join" with his daughter and come along-side her to problem solve.

Write down a memory you might have of going to your parent(s) with a problem or question, and having a similar conversation to the one between Sally and her father:

_____

_____

_____

_____

_____

_____

_____

How do you think this made you feel?

_____

_____

_____

_____

How do you think this changed how you felt about yourself?

_____

_____

_____

_____

_____

Was there another parent or adult that you could talk to about your problems that was emotionally accessible to you? What do you remember about them? How were they different?

_____

_____

_____

_____

_____

_____

_____

How do you think this person helped you to see yourself differently?

_____

_____

_____

_____

_____

Write down any thoughts or feelings you have about how your family communicated when you were a child:

_____

_____

_____

_____

_____

In covertly narcissistic families, communication appears to be for the good of the children and gives them the impression that the parents only want what is best for them. The direction of any conversation, however, if you look closely, is always away from the child and towards the parent in order to make them look good. Conversations are not give and take, they usually make children feel bad about *who they are* as opposed to *what they did*, and leave them feeling lonely and invisible. Either communication is one-sided (keep in mind the analogy of the mirror) or in many cases there is simply no parent available to have a conversation with. They might be around and home doing all the things that good parents do around the house for their family, but like Gertrude Stein once said: "There's no there, there." They expect empathy, attention and understanding, but are simply incapable of giving those things to their children on a consistent basis. I say consistently because I do not believe anything is "always" or "never" but as you explore the dynamics of a covertly narcissistic family, think in terms of "most of the time." Children who grow up in this type of system learn to cling to the exceptions rather than the rule because it helped them survive. As adults, unfortunately, this survival skill keeps them in unhealthy relationships that are eerily as one-sided and dysfunctional as the one they grew up in.

"

"I used to spend so much time reacting and responding to everyone else that my life had no direction. Other people's lives, problems, and wants set the course for my life. Once I realized it was okay for me to think about and identify what I wanted, remarkable things began to take place in my life."
— *Melody Beattie, The Language of Letting Go: Hazelden Meditation Series*

The following quote is a real example that encapsulates every dysfunctional communication style in a covertly narcissistic family. I added it to the end of the chapter so that it wasn't distracting, but in case you are unsure whether people really do this to their children, read how one mother describes why she is selling her daughter's One Direction concert tickets on Ebay. This is the complete ad—all the CAPS are where she had them (which is like cyber yelling) and all the grammar, etc. has been left as is. Keep in mind that the average age of a One Direction (a boy band for all of you without teen aged girls!) is around 13 years old. I'm not going to analyze this for you, but I will say that this got a lot of "atta girl" comments from people who read the same article I did.

"This auction is for all 4 one direction tickets in Sydney October 25. You can thank my daughters lippy attitude for their sale. See sweety? And you thought I was bluffing. I hope the scowl on your bitchy little friends faces when you tell them that your dad and I revoked the gift we were giving you all reminds you that your PARENTS are the ones that deserve love and respect more than anyone. And your silly little pack mentality of taking your parents for fools is one sadly mistaken. Anyhow. Your loss is someone else's gain who deserves them! THE TICKETS ARE SEATED IN ROW O section 57. REMEMBER AUCTION IS FOR ALL 4 TICKETS and will be sent registered post.

...OH YOUR FRIENDS THOUGHT THAT A FEW PRANK CALLS WOULD PUT ME OFF SELLING THE GIFT WE BOUGHT THEM for YOUR BIRTHDAY because YOU all LIED to us about sleep overs so you could hang like little trollops at and older guys HOUSE???? Pffft!! I find it HIGHLY amusing that you girls think you invented this stuff. Tricks like this on OUR parents is how HALF of you were conceived...And why a lot of your friends DON'T have and address to send that Fathers day card to!!! I'm not your friend. I'm your MOTHER. And I am here to give you the boundaries that YOU NEED to become a functional responsible adult. You may hate me now...But I don't care. Its my job to raise a responsible adult...not nurture bad habits in my teen age child."

"Experience has taught us that we have only one enduring weapon in our struggle against mental illness: the emotional discovery and emotional acceptance of the truth in the individual and unique history of our childhood."
— *Alice Miller, The Drama of the Gifted Child: The Search for the True Self*

PART II: THE PRESENT

Chapter 4:

Understanding Codependency

Codependency is one of those words that seems to have many meanings depending on who you talk to or what book you are reading. For adult children of covert narcissists, codependency is very subtle and hard to detect unless you have "been there." Many think of a codependent person as someone who just does not have a backbone—a doormat—a wet noodle who doesn't have her own mind. An Edith Bunker (google it if you have no idea who I am talking about). Or maybe a codependent is a wife who picks up her drunk husband from the bar for the 100th time and tries to make him quit by pouring his whiskey down the sink. It can look like those two examples, and often does, but there are many, less obvious ways that codependency works in relationships. To make it simple, codependency describes a relationship where one person is doing all the giving, and the other person is doing all the taking. It's a pattern of intimacy that begins in childhood and can continue far into adulthood. Taking care of someone at the expense of meeting your own needs in order to feel loved and needed doesn't work—ever. It's not an easy process to begin to deal with codependent tendencies, nor is it fun to take an honest look at the consequences of putting yourself last. Most people, no matter what age, feel angry when they have their "light bulb" moment and realize that they are, in fact, codependent. Elizabeth Kubler-Ross outlined five stages of grieving: denial, anger, bargaining, depression, and acceptance. Seeing the truth about things in our lives that have been going on for years is like experiencing a death—you might find yourself going through the stages of grieving to some extent. The fantasy of what the relationship should/could have been is gone. As painful as this "death" is, and it is painful, it does allow new, healthy relationships to form.

Although adult children of covert narcissists do share many of these characteristics, they face challenges that are unique to them, which will be explained later in this chapter. These are some of the behaviors that adult children of alcoholics struggle with that may feel familiar to people raised in narcissistic families:

- approval seeking

- being frightened of angry people and criticism

- loss of identity

- super responsible or super irresponsible

- victim behavior

- fear of abandonment

- feel guilty when expressing needs/wants

- rescuers

- reactors rather than actors in life

- put the needs of others first

- avoid confrontation

- often feel angry but afraid to express it

- attracted to people that need help

- have difficulty having fun

- start things but don't finish them

- loyal even when people don't deserve loyalty

- impulsive

- judge themselves without mercy

- afraid of authority

- difficulty with intimacy

- issues with money

- tendency to isolate when overwhelmed

Did any of the items on the list stand out to you more than the others? What were they?

_____

_____

_____

_____

How has this behavior affected your life and relationships?

_____

_____

_____

_____

_____

_____

Which items did not apply to you?

_____

_____

_____

_____

_____

Why?

_____

_____

_____

_____

_____

"No" is a complete sentence.
— Anne Lamott

"One thing: you have to walk, and create the way by your walking; you will not find a ready-made path. It is not so cheap, to reach to the ultimate realization of truth. You will have to create the path by walking yourself; the path is not ready-made, lying there and waiting for you. It is just like the sky: the birds fly, but they don't leave any footprints. You cannot follow them; there are no footprints left behind."
— *Osho*

Chapter 5

Understanding Adult Children of Narcissists

Adult children of narcissists and adult children of alcoholics both grew up in homes where the needs of the parents came before the needs of the child, and they share many personality and behavioral traits because of the way they were raised. Some of the behaviors common in people who were raised by narcissistic parents are:

- a chronic need to please

- difficulty identifying feelings, wants and needs

- a constant need for validation

- difficulty being assertive

- feel like they deserve the bad things that happen to them

- feelings of rage that they are afraid of

- difficulty with intimacy and trust

- either distrustful or disclose too much

- feeling of emptiness and dissatisfaction

- inability to make clear decisions

- afraid to ask for what they need

- isolate when they feel inadequate or overwhelmed

- never feel like they're working hard enough or doing enough

Notice the codependent similarities? For many adult children of narcissists, these feelings or behaviors may be a very well-kept secret—most people you know would be shocked that you struggle in these areas. Well, maybe not, but you try your hardest to cover up the areas in your life that might give people the impression that you aren't totally on top of things. There is a great deal of shame around these characteristics, but what you need to understand, and learn to accept, is that they were *learned* behaviors. And if they were learned, they can be unlearned. For that to happen, the first thing that needs to go is the amount of debilitating shame that comes along with not having it all together. Here's a shocker, and you might want to sit down before you read this, but I have to tell you the truth: No one has it all together. No one. Zero. I don't care how they dress, or the job they have, how perfect their children seem, their amazingly wonderful spouse, or their perfect bodies. Everyone screws up, everyone has problems, and you're not the only one you know who feels like they missed the boat somewhere along the line. Now that I've cleared that up, let's look at what's going on in your life right now.

To help you better understand how growing up in a narcissistic family has affected you as an adult, I created an assessment tool that incorporates codependency traits from the Codependency List, a list of criteria in the DSM-5 for NPD, elements listed in the NPI-16 and the Hypersensitivity

Scale (HSNS). Assessments are useful because they help pinpoint certain patterns or themes that pertain specifically to your life, your experience and your particular circumstances. Not everything in every assessment will pertain to you at this moment in your life; there may be things that really do not affect you very much, but others that seem to be a pervasive issue in your life. These assessments are not meant to answer all your questions or sum up your life in a nutshell; they are really designed to help you see your life a little more objectively so you can begin the process of healing.

Adult Children of Covert Narcissists Assessment (McDonald, 2013)

Please check the answer that most closely describes you right now:

1.	a) _____ I am afraid of and avoid authority figures. b) _____ Authority figures don't bother me.
2.	a) _____ I often don't say what I think in order to keep the peace. b) _____ I feel free to speak my own mind even if people don't agree with me.
3.	a) _____ I try to avoid making people angry with me. b) _____ I know that sometimes people might get angry with me, although I would prefer that they don't.
4.	a) _____ I am afraid of being criticized or judged. b) _____ I don't like being criticized or judged, but I am not afraid of it.
5.	a) _____ I feel guilty if I make a mistake. b) _____ I know that everyone makes mistakes, even me.
6.	a) _____ I have had more than one relationship where I give love, but don't get much in return. b) _____ My relationships are generally equal as far as giving and receiving love.

7.	a) _____ It's easy for me to show empathy and understanding, but I often feel lonely and misunderstood. b) _____ I feel empathy from and understood by the people I love.
8.	a) _____ I feel responsible if things go wrong, even if it's not my fault. b) _____ I don't always feel responsible if thing so wrong.
9.	a) _____ My life feels chaotic and out of control most of the time. b) _____ Some days are hectic, but most days my life feels stable.
10.	a) _____ I feel anxious around people most of the time. b) _____ I rarely feel anxious around people.
11.	a) _____ I am the one people come to for help with their problems. b) _____ My friends and family have healthy support systems.
12.	a) _____ I have trouble putting myself first. b) _____ I take good care of myself.
13.	a) _____ I rarely ask for help. b) _____ If I need help I ask for it.
14.	a) _____ I often say "yes" when I mean "no." b) _____ I am able to say "no" to people.
15.	a) _____ I do not feel emotionally supported by people closest to me. b) _____ I feel emotionally supported by the people closest to me.

| 16. | c) _____ I often start things, but don't finish them. |
| | d) _____ I set goals and complete tasks. |

Totals: _____ (a) _____ (b)

Adult children of narcissistic parents would answer more questions with (a) then they would with (b).

Choose three of the questions you answered with (a) and write down any thoughts or feelings you have about them:

1.

_____

_____

_____

2.

_____

_____

_____

3.

_____

_____

_____

For adult children of narcissists, there's a general feeling of loneliness, depression, unhealthy or destructive relationship patterns, lack of involvement in the community (isolation), anxiety, unfulfilled dreams, and a constant feeling that something is missing. They're talented, bright, and sometimes gifted, but cannot seem to "get it together" for one reason or another. Alice Miller (1981) wrote that gifted children seem to bear the brunt of their narcissistic parent's rage most profoundly, perhaps because they trigger feelings of inadequacy or threaten the narcissists fragile ego the most.

What talents have gone unrealized because of the abuse suffered by children who are made to feel inherently flawed? Getting healthy isn't a matter of becoming something else or changing who you are. It is really a process of examining beliefs about who you are, figuring out where those beliefs came from and deciding what works and what does not. What is real? What ideas about yourself were handed to you that you never questioned? Are you really lazy? Really? Accepting the image of who you are that was projected onto you by a narcissistic parent can keep you from discovering what an amazing human being you are and living the life you were meant to live.

"Healing is impossible in loneliness; it is the opposite of loneliness. Conviviality is healing. To be healed we must come with all the other creatures to the feast of Creation."
——Wendell Berry, The Art of the Commonplace: The Agrarian Essays

"Be who you are and say what you
feel, because those who mind don't
matter, and those who matter don't
mind."
— Bernard M. Baruch

Chapter 6

Understanding Yourself as a Separate Individual

One of the most difficult things for an adult children of narcissists to do in the healing

process is to begin the journey (and it is a journey, so be patient) of separating themselves as

individuals from their parents. A hallmark of a narcissistic family system is that children are not

allowed to express their true feelings or be who they want to be. They develop a "false self" that's

acceptable and reflects the image that makes their parents feel good about themselves. The true self

is buried deep within, it doesn't go anywhere, but it's suppressed because it's unacceptable. Much of

the behavior that comes out of codependency stems from trying to live out of that mirror image.

There are some elements of the true self that remain, but they're just pieces. To be fully alive and

truly become healthy as opposed to perfect, it's essential to discover, accept and learn to love

yourself on your own terms, as your own person. Easier said than done, right? How do you get to

know someone you left behind in childhood, someone you learned to hide, maybe even dislike?

One of the most amazing tools that I have discovered to help people identify their personality types is called the Enneagram. I'm not going to go into the history too much in this workbook because it's quite involved, but if you are interested in learning about it more in depth, I have listed some resources in the back of the book. It is really a fascinating subject. Briefly, the theory behind the Enneagram is that we are all born with a predominant personality that determines how we will react to our environment. There are nine types that use numbers, they apply to both men and women, no number is better than another, and although we all have a little bit of each personality type, we all born with a dominant type that we operate out of. That number is what we are going to focus on.

The following test is from the Enneagram Institute (2010) and is a quick version of their Enneagram sorter. The Quest is not 100% accurate, it's designed to get you started on the journey of discovering your type, but it isn't definitive. Remember, don't over-think it, just report what feels most accurate for you.

QUEST: QUICK ENNEAGRAM SORTING TEST

GROUP I

Rate: _____

A. I have tended to be fairly independent and assertive: I've felt that life works best when you meet it head-on. I set my own goals, get involved, and want to make things happen. I don't like sitting around—I want to achieve something big and have an impact. I don't necessarily seek confrontations, but I don't let people push me around either. Most of the time, I know what I want and I go for it. I tend to work hard and to play hard.

Rate: _____

B. I have tended to be quiet and am used to being on my own. I usually don't draw much attention to myself socially, and it's generally unusual for me to assert myself all that forcefully. I don't feel comfortable taking the lead or being as competitive as others. Many would probably say that I'm something of a dreamer—a lot of my excitement goes on in my imagination. I can be quite content without feeling I have to be active all the time.

Rate: _____

C. I have tended to be extremely responsible and dedicated. I feel terrible if I don't keep my commitments and do what's expected of me. I want people to know that I'm there for them and that I'll do what I believe is best for them. I've often made great personal sacrifices for the sake of others, whether they know it or not. I often don't take adequate care of myself—I do the work that needs to be done and relax (and do what I want) if there's time left.

GROUP II

Rate: _____

X. I am a person who usually maintains a positive outlook and feels that things will work out for the best. I can usually find something to be enthusiastic about and different ways to occupy myself. I like being around people and helping others be happy—I enjoy sharing my own well-being with them. (I don't always feel great, but I generally try not to show it!) However, keeping a positive frame of mind has sometimes meant that I've put off dealing with my own problems for too long.

Rate: _____

Y. I am a person who has strong feelings about things—most people can tell when I'm upset about something. I can be guarded with people, but I'm more sensitive than I let on. I want to know where I stand with others and who and what I can count on—it's pretty clear to most people where they stand with me. When I'm upset about something, I want others to respond and to get as worked up as I am. I know the rules, but I don't want people telling me what to do. I want to decide for myself.

Rate: _____

Z. I am a person who is self-controlled and logical—I don't like revealing my feelings or getting bogged down in them. I am efficient—even perfectionistic—about my work, and prefer working on my own. If there are problems or personal conflicts, I try not to let my feelings influence my actions. Some say I'm too cool and detached, but I don't want my private reactions to distract me from what's really important. I'm glad that I usually don't show my reactions when other's "get to me."

Instructions:

Rate the paragraphs in each Group from 3 to 1, with "3" being the one that *best describes your actual behavior now*.

Then match the letters on the table below and add your weights to find what the three most probable candidates for your personality type are. For example, one type will be most probable with the highest score of "6" for most agreement in both Groups.

2-digit code	Type
AX	7
AY	8
AZ	3
BX	9
BY	4
BZ	5
CX	2
CY	6
CZ	1

My Type: _____

My Enneagram

Number: _____

The Nine Personality Types of the Enneagram

1. **The Reformer.** *The principled, idealistic type.* Ones are conscientious and ethical with a strong sense of right and wrong. They are teachers, crusaders, and advocates for change: always striving to improve things, but afraid of making a mistake. Well-organized, orderly, and fastidious, they try to maintain high standards, but can slip into being critical and perfectionistic. They typically have problems with resentment and impatience. At their best: wise, discerning, realistic, and noble. Can be morally heroic.

2. **The Helper.** *The caring, interpersonal type.* Twos are empathic, sincere, and warm-hearted. They are friendly, generous, and self-sacrificing, but can also be sentimental, flattering, and people-pleasing. They are well-meaning and driven to be close to others, but can slip into doing things for others in order to be needed. They typically have problems with possessiveness and with acknowledging their own needs. At their best: unselfish and altruistic, they have unconditional love for others.

3. **The Achiever.** *The adaptable, success-oriented type.* Threes are self-assured, attractive, and charming. Ambitious, competent, and energetic, they can also be status-conscious and highly driven for advancement. They are diplomatic and poised, but can also be overly concerned with their image and what others think of them. They typically have problems with workaholism and competitiveness. At their best: self-accepting, authentic, everything they seem to be—role models who inspire others.

4. **The Individualist.** *The introspective, romantic type.* Fours are self-aware, sensitive, and reserved. They are emotionally honest, creative, and personal, but can also be moody and self-conscious. Withholding themselves from others due to feeling vulnerable and defective, they can also feel disdainful and exempt from ordinary ways of living. They typically have problems with melancholy, self-indulgence, and self-pity. At their best: inspired and highly creative, they are able to renew themselves and transform their experiences.

5. **The Investigator.** *The perceptive, cerebral type.* Fives are alert, insightful, and curious. They are able to concentrate and focus on developing complex ideas and skills. Independent, innovative, and inventive, they can also become preoccupied with their thoughts and imaginary constructs. They become detached, yet high-strung and intense. They typically have problems with eccentricity, nihilism, and isolation. At their best: visionary pioneers, often ahead of their time, and able to see the world in an entirely new way.

6. **The Loyalist.** *The committed, security-oriented type.* Sixes are reliable, hard-working, responsible, and trustworthy. Excellent "troubleshooters," they foresee problems and foster cooperation, but can also become defensive, evasive and anxious—running on stress while complaining about it. They can be cautious and indecisive, but also reactive, defiant and rebellious. They typically have problems with self-doubt and suspicion. At their best: internally stable and self-reliant, courageously championing themselves and others.

7. **The Enthusiast.** *The busy, productive type.* Sevens are extroverted, optimistic, versatile, and spontaneous. Playful, high-spirited, and practical, they can also misapply their many talents, becoming over-extended, scattered, and undisciplined. They constantly seek new and exciting experiences, but can become distracted and exhausted by staying on the go. They typically have problems with impatience and impulsiveness. At their best: they focus their talents on worthwhile goals, becoming appreciative, joyous, and satisfied.

8. **The Challenger.** *The powerful, aggressive type.* Eights are self-confident, strong, and assertive. Protective, resourceful, straight-talking, and decisive, but can also be ego-centric and domineering. Eights feel they must control their environment, especially people, sometimes becoming confrontational and intimidating. Eights typically have problems with their tempers and with allowing themselves to be vulnerable. At their best: self-mastering, they use their strength to improve others' lives, becoming heroic, magnanimous, and inspiring.

9. **The Peacemaker.** *The easy-going, self-effacing type.* Nines are accepting, trusting, and stable. They are usually grounded, supportive, and often creative, but can also be too willing to go along with others to keep the peace. They want everything to go smoothly and be without conflict, but they can also tend to be complacent and emotionally distant, simplifying problems and ignoring anything upsetting. They typically have problems with inertia and stubbornness. At their best: indomitable and all-embracing, they are able to bring people together and heal conflicts.

Write down your thoughts about your top type scores on the Enneagram:

_____

_____

_____

_____

_____

From these top types, what have you learned about what your strengths might be?

_____

_____

_____

_____

What have you learned about what some of your weaknesses might be?

_____

_____

_____

_____

Everyone has natural, inborn strengths and weaknesses. According to the theory of the Enneagram, we all have a tendency to retreat into certain behaviors when we feel stress and also a way that we behave when things are going really well. Each type has these two correlating behaviors that are neither good or bad, they are just tendencies. Rather than thinking of your weaknesses as negative, think of them as a signal that you aren't taking care of yourself, or not dealing with something that needs your attention. You will begin to notice patterns—what you do when you're feeling great, or what might trigger you to go into less productive behaviors. Growing is about understanding yourself and learning how to operate out of your strengths while managing your weaknesses. Do you hide in your room when you feel overwhelmed? Well, that is perfectly fine for a short period of time, but it's important to figure out what is overwhelming you so that you can face it and get back to doing what you need to be doing. Maybe when you get tired you get bossy and act like a little dictator, or start to cry for no apparent reason. Fine, that's you. Instead of feeling ashamed or hating that part of you, learn to use it and to respect it. You want be your best self, and not live out of that aspect of your personality, or use it as a defense mechanism. How can your weaknesses work for you and not against you? Nobody is perfect, including you, so accepting that is first and foremost, but once you get a grasp of that truth and begin the process of loving the "even not so great" parts of you personality, then what? Well, then we take a look at what needs to change in your life in order to begin that wonderful journey towards authenticity. How can your outer life begin to reflect your newly emerging inner self? That's the goal: to really live life on your own terms, and embrace it. Life isn't easy, that's a given, but it can be yours to experience consciously and with courage. You can face challenges, you are fully capable of overcoming obstacles, and you have so much to offer the world. There is only one you! Let us now take a look at what you want to change and where to start.

God grant me the serenity to accept the
things I cannot change, the courage to
change the things I can, and the wisdom to
know the difference.
—Reinhold Niebuhr

"We did not come here to fear the future, we came here to shape it."

—Barack Obama

PART III: THE FUTURE

Chapter 7

Understanding Change

Change is difficult. Where do you begin? Well, at the beginning is a nice place to start and it does not have to be anything monumental. It can be, and I'm not going to discourage any acts of amazing bravery if you feel like you're ready for that! However, generally speaking, change is very scary and people can set themselves up to fail when they over-estimate what they're honestly ready to tackle. Small steps really do add up and before you know it, you are miles from where you started, but it was manageable and the changes you made to get there will last. This next exercise is called **The Life Pie** and it helps you become more aware of what is working in your life and what may not be going so well, and where you want to make some changes. It is a great way to step back and gain some perspective on your life, so you can decide where you want to focus your energy right now. Like all really useful exercises, it is short and simple, but very useful in helping narrow down one small area that can make a huge difference in how you are living.

Instructions:

In each of the eight sections write down the most important aspects of your life. For example: "love," "family," "career," "school," etc. After you have filled out each of the eight sections, rank each area from zero to ten:

- 10 means: "This part of my life is absolutely great, I would not change a thing."
- 0 means: "This part of my life it totally unacceptable to me and it exhausts me."
- 5 means: "I'm OK with this aspect of my life, it isn't great, but it isn't horrible."

EXAMPLE:

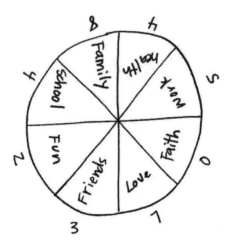

Choose one area you'd like to work on and make another pie separated into eight more slices with the title: "WORK" or whatever area you chose. Write different "tasks" you can work on to improve that area of your life and rate each task from 0-10 based on what you feel is most important or "do-able" right now.

EXAMPLE:

Based on your ratings, choose a task you'd like to get started on. If you want to break down that task even more, just make another pie and divide it into two or more manageable pieces.

LIFE PIE:

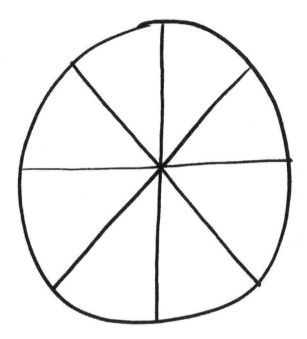

Choose the task you'd like to work on and divide it into manageable pieces:

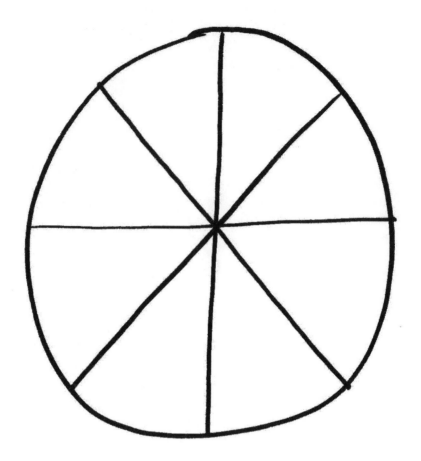

Make a list of what you plan to do and a deadline:

1. _____ date: _____

2. _____ date: _____

3. _____ date: _____

4. _____ date: _____

5. _____ date: _____

6. _____ date: _____

7. _____ date: _____

8. _____ date: _____

"There is nothing like returning to a
place that remains unchanged to
find the ways in which you yourself
have altered."
— *Nelson Mandela*

Chapter 8

Understanding Conflict

For adult children of narcissists, establishing and creating healthy boundaries often involves

some sort of confrontation because it means standing up for yourself, and we all know how fun that

is for codependents! Boundaries are like fences, and you can't keep moving them around every time

someone wants you to, then get mad because people don't understand where they can and can't go.

As you've gotten to know yourself through the course of this workbook, you are (hopefully) more

aware of what you need, how you feel, and what some of your triggers are. How do you ask for what

you want? How do you tell someone—who might get mad at you (but maybe not, you ever know)—

that you don't want something, or that you aren't going to do what they want? Confrontation means

different things to different people, but it doesn't have to mean a screaming match, or involve door

slamming. The Merriam-Webster Dictionary defines confrontation as: "discord resulting from a

clash of ideas or opinions." For codependents, this can mean saying they would rather go get ice

cream than pie, or they really don't like baseball even though they said they did. It could also mean something more serious like confronting a doctor, or having a dispute with the bank about their investments. Confrontation styles are like snowflakes—no two are alike—but people do fall into certain categories to some extent. Understanding your particular confrontation style may help you feel more in control, so that setting boundaries won't feel as intimidating. Gaining insight into how you confront conflict is another step in accepting who you are, being honest, dealing with issues as they come up, and asking for what you need in a way that's respectful.

Can you think of a recent conflict or confrontation you had recently? What were the circumstances?

_____

_____

_____

_____

How did you handle it?

_____

_____

_____

_____

How do you wish you had handled it?

_____

_____

_____

_____

_____

_____

CONFLICT STRATEGIES: WHAT ARE YOU LIKE?

Different people use different strategies for managing conflict. These strategies are learned in childhood, and seem to function automatically. Usually we aren't aware at the time of how we act in conflict situations; we do whatever seems to come naturally. But, we do have a personal strategy; and because it was learned, we can always change it by learning new and more effective way of managing conflicts.

When you become engaged in a conflict, there are two major concerns you have to take into account:

1. Achieving your personal goals: You are in conflict because you have a goal that conflicts with another person's goals. Your goal may be highly important to you, or it may be of little importance.

2. Keeping good relationship with another person: You may need to be able to interact effectively with the other person in the future. The relationship may be very important to you, or it may be of little importance.

The importance of these two areas will affect the ways in which you act in any given confrontation.

"The only thing we have to fear, is fear itself."
—Franklin D. Roosevelt

CONFLICT STYLE QUESTIONNAIRE:

How do you act when you need to confront someone or experience conflict in your relationships? The sayings listed in the following questionnaire can be thought of as some of the different strategies for resolving conflict. Read each of the sayings and using the following scale, score how typical each is of your actions when in conflict:

1. Never do this.   2. Seldom do this.   3. Sometimes do this.   4. Frequently do this.   5. Usually do this.

	SCORE
1. It's easier to refrain than to retreat from a quarrel.	1.
2. If you can't make a person think as you do, make him do as you think.	2.
3. Soft words win hearts.	3.
4. You scratch my back, I'll scratch yours.	4.
5. Come now and let's reason together.	5.
6. When two people argue, the person who keeps silent is the most praiseworthy.	6.
7. Might overcomes right.	7.
8. Smooth words make smooth ways.	8.
9. Better half a loaf than no bread at all.	9.
10. Truth lies in knowledge, not in majority opinion.	10.
11. He who fights and runs away lives to fight another day.	11.
12. He has conquered well that has made his enemies flee.	12.

13. Kill 'em with kindness.	13.
14. A fair exchange brings no quarrel.	14.
15. No person has the final answer, but every person has a piece to contribute.	15.
16. Stay away from people who disagree with you.	16.
17. Fields are won by those who believe in winning.	17.
18. Kind words are worth much and cost little.	18.
19. You get me, I'll get you back.	19.
20. Only the person who is willing to give up having to be right can learn from the wisdom of others.	20.
21. Avoid quarrelsome people as they will only make your life miserable.	21.
22. Kind words are worth much and cost little.	22.
23. Soft words ensure harmony.	23.
24. One gift for another makes good friends.	24.
25. Bring your conflicts into the open and face them directly; only then will the best solution be discovered.	25.
26. The best way of handling conflict is to avoid them.	26.
27. Put your foot down where you mean to stand.	27.
28. Gentleness will triumph over anger.	28.
29. Getting part of what you want is better than not getting anything at all.	29.
30. Frankness, honesty and trust will move mountains.	30.
31. There is nothing so important you have to fight for it.	31.
32. There are two kinds of people in the world, the winners and the losers.	32.

33. When one hits you with a stone, hit him or her with a piece of cotton.	33.
34. When both give in halfway, a fair settlement is achieved.	34.
35. By digging and digging, the truth is discovered.	35.

SCORING:

- Copy your scorings from the questionnaire into the table below.
- Total the columns.
- The higher the total score for each strategy, the more frequently you tend to use that approach.

withdrawing		forcing		smoothing		compromising		confronting	
1		2		3		4		5	
6		7		8		9		10	
11		12		13		14		15	
16		17		18		19		20	
21		22		23		24		25	
26		27		28		29		30	
31		32		33		34		35	
total		total		total		total		Total	

For an explanation of each type see the following "type chart."

TYPES:

	THE TURTLE (WITHDRAWING): Turtles withdraw into their shells to avoid conflicts. They give up their personal goals and relationships. They stay away from the issues over which the conflict is taking place and from the persons they are in conflict with. Turtles believe it is hopeless to try and resolve conflicts. They feel helpless. They believe it is easier to withdraw (physically and psychologically) from a conflict than to face it. **STRENGTH:** Calm on the outside and realize most conflicts solve themselves. Able to de-escalate volatile situations. Peacemakers.
	THE SHARK (FORCING): Sharks try to overpower opponents by forcing them to accept their solutions to the conflict. Their goals are highly important to them and relationships of minor importance. They seek to achieve their goals at all costs. They aren't concerned with needs of others. They don't care if others like or accept them. Sharks assume that conflicts are neither won nor lost and they want to be the winner. They try to win by attacking, overpowering, or overwhelming and intimidating others. **STRENGTHS:** Strong and courageous, natural leaders, and will confront injustice head on.
	THE TEDDY BEAR (SMOOTHING): To Teddy Bears, the relationship is of great importance while their own goals are of little importance. Teddies want to be accepted and liked by other people. The think that conflict should be avoided in favor of harmony and that people can't discuss conflicts without damaging relationships. They're afraid that if a conflict continues, someone will get hurt and that could ruin the relationship. They like to smooth things over. **STRENGTHS:** This is the most loveable and likeable person in most situations. They are able to bring peace and harmony to the most difficult conflicts through their natural insight and compassion.
	THE FOX (COMPROMISING): Foxes are moderately concerned with their own goals and their relationships with others. They seek a conflict solution in which both sides gain something—the middle ground. They compromise; they will give up a part of their goal and relationship in order to find agreement for the common good. Foxes can be manipulative and deceptive. **STRENGTHS:** They are very crafty in coming up with creative solutions to complicated interpersonal problems.

 **THE OWL (CONFRONTING):** Owls highly value their own goals and relationships. They view conflicts as problems to be solved and seek a solution that achieves both their own and the other person's goals. Owls see conflicts as a means of improving relationships by reducing tension between two people. By seeking solutions that satisfy everyone, owls maintain the relationship. They are not good when a quick solution must be found and have to have two willing parties for this style to work. Sometimes idealistic and expect others to operate with the same integrity. **STRENGTHS:** Do not have to have things their way, very open-minded and willing to share their wisdom. Very practical.

As in all things, nothing is "always" one way and "never" another, but we do have particular ways that we tend to behave when we feel overwhelmed, or threatened that we might not be aware of. When you're feeling good and on top of things, dealing with conflict might come easily to you—you aren't a turtle, you're a fierce shark! However, those moments might be the exception rather than the rule. When we talk about confrontation styles, we want to look at "the norm;" how you respond most of the time. Like we talked about with the Enneagram types, no style is good and no style is bad; each has its own particular strengths and its own weaknesses. What is important is for you to recognize is that your way of coping does have a plus side if you learn to use it for the greater good, and not to use it to hide behind or defend yourself, but as a way of contributing. A shark is an awesome ally when being his or her best, but a terrible foe when cornered or frightened. A wise old owl is great to have when you need to sit down and really examine a trick situation from all angles, but maybe not so great in the middle of a bar fight. What is really wonderful, and truthfully the goal of understanding and accepting yourself, is when you begin to realize other people have strengths and weaknesses as well.

What are the weaknesses of your confrontation style?

_____

_____

_____

_____

_____

Can you think of a conflict in the recent past where you responded this way?

_____

_____

_____

_____

What are the strengths of you confrontation style?

_____

_____

_____

_____

Can you think of a conflict in the recent past where you responded this way?

_____

_____

_____

_____

Does your conflict style correspond with your Enneagram type? In what way or not?

_____

_____

_____

_____

_____

What is the one thing you could do to deal better with conflict?

_____

_____

_____

_____

Is there a situation that you are dealing with now that involves confrontation? Explain:

_____

_____

_____

_____

How could you use what you have learned so far to ask for what you need, express your feelings or set healthy boundaries in this situation?

_____

_____

_____

_____

"We change our behavior when the pain of staying the same becomes greater than the pain of changing. Consequences give us the pain that motivates us to change."
— Henry Cloud

"Twenty years from now you will be
more disappointed by the things that
you didn't do than by the ones you
did do. So throw off the bowlines.
Sail away from the safe harbor.
Catch the trade winds in your sails.
Explore. Dream. Discover."
— *H. Jackson Brown Jr.*

Chapter 9

Understanding Dreams and Desires

Everyone loves to read about people who take amazing risks and end up being successful beyond their wildest dreams. Some lady discovers a great way to redesign a stroller one day while walking her kids in the park and sells her idea and is now a bazillionaire. I don't know how that happens, and I don't know anyone personally who is successful that hasn't had to work like crazy to get there. I'm not just talking about making money here, I'm talking about feeling excited about what you do, and waking up most days feeling like you have a purpose in life. Money is great, don't get me wrong. If you've ever been even a little poor you know just how much better having money is. But, it isn't everything. Money can own you, can keep you stuck in relationships and jobs that make you miserable because the fear or not having it is overwhelmingly terrifying. It can control you because it says to the world (or to your narcissistic parents) that you're good enough, that you're what they either said you would be or what they expected from you all along. Are you dissatisfied because you hate what you're doing? Maybe you're a kindergarten teacher who always wanted to be a doctor, or a truck driver who always dreamed of being a floral designer. Who knows? How do you discern what your dreams and desires are, and what was chosen for you by default?

THE PERFECT DAY EXERCISE

This exercise is called The Perfect Day. It is a great little tool that helps you become more in tune with what makes you happy, what your values are, what is important to you, and what your dreams and desires might really be.

Instructions: Write (in detail) what your perfect day would look like from the time you get up, until the time you go to bed. If you could live any life you wanted to live, what would it look like? Where would you live? Who would you live with? Do you have a cat or dog? Be as detailed as you can, have fun with this exercise, but also write down a real life. I know, it would be really cool to ride a unicorn to work and have a time machine, but I want you to be as honest as you can be with what you truly want, and what truly matters to you. Feel free to use your journal or a ream of paper if you need to:

My Perfect day would start out with:

_____

_____

_____

_____

_____

_____

_____

_____

_____

_____

_____

Values List Exercise:

From your Perfect Day Exercise, underline the values listed below that reflect what drives you, what you enjoy, inspires you, and that you would like more of. By building a life and lifestyle around our values, we create a life that is more satisfying and meaningful to us. Values can change over time, and deepen as you understand yourself better—they are always moving. Your values can also be situational, so what is true for you at work may not be true for you at home. Finally, the Values List below is ONLY to give you some ideas of examples or sample values. We are each unique, so there will be words that are missing from this list, and different words that sum up your values better. If so, feel free to add those words to the list below.

VALUES LIST:

Accomplishment	Accuracy	Affection
Adventure	Authenticity	Art
Balance	Beauty	Boldness
Calm	Carefree	Challenge
Children	Community	Comfort
Confidence	Companionship	Contentment
Connectedness	Confidence	Creativity
Determination	Drive	Direction
Empowerment	Energy	Excitement
Environment	Excellence	Fairness

Faith	Family	Freedom
Fun	Generosity	Growth
Happiness	Harmony	Health
Honesty	Honor	Humor
Integrity	Intuition	Joy
Kindness	Learning	Listening
Loving	Loyalty	Money
Nature	Optimism	Orderliness
Perfection	Peace	Patience
Passion	Productivity	Recognition
Respect	Resourcefulness	Romance
Safety	Security	Self-esteem
Service	Simplicity	Spirituality
Spontaneity	Strength	thankfulness
Tolerance	Trust	Tradition
Understanding	Unity	Wisdom

Is there anything you would like to change about your life to be more in line with your values? If so, what would you change?

_____

_____

_____

_____

Are there areas in your life where you're living according to your values? If so, what did you do to make that happen?

_____

_____

_____

_____

_____

Adult children of narcissists learn early on what their parents values are, and accept many of them as if they were their own. Perhaps your Dad was a lawyer, and his Dad was a lawyer, does that mean you have to be a lawyer too? Living according to another person's value system is not only dissatisfying, but it's a huge waste of talent. If some doesn't really want to be a lawyer, chances are they aren't a very good one. When you discover your passion in life, and pursue that dream, it won't be easy to break with what has been expected of you, but there is nothing better than working in "your sweet spot." You benefit, and society benefits. I don't know about you, but if I need a lawyer, I want to hire one who really loves being one!

It's never too late to change, and there is no situation that can't be adjusted. You may not be able to quit your job tomorrow and join the circus, but if you really wanted to be a circus clown, you could find a class and start there. Brainstorm ways that you can incorporate you values and dreams into your everyday life. We can always find excuses, but if that same energy was poured into looking for possibilities, all kinds of fun things can happen. Use your LIFE PIE tool to problem solve, and come up with ideas that are do-able. Sure, there will be people who tell you that your ideas will never work, and all of the reasons why, but what are they doing with their lives? Consider the source. Use your conflict style to work around Uncle Billy who tells you at the family reunion how one of his buddies tried that and ended up losing his house and going insane. If you look, you will find people who support you, encourage you, and believe in you. Find them.

"There is only one thing that makes a dream impossible to achieve: the fear of failure."
Paulo Coelho, The Alchemist

"What is home? My favorite definition is "a safe place," a place where one is free from attack, a place where one experiences secure relationships and affirmation. It's a place where people share and understand each other. Its relationships are nurturing. The people in it do not need to be perfect; instead, they need to be honest, loving, supportive, recognizing a common humanity that makes all of us vulnerable."
— Gladys Hunt, *Honey for a Child's Heart: The Imaginative Use of Books in Family Life*

Chapter 10

Understanding Support and Community

Adult children of covert narcissists are either over-involved in their communities—super helpers that do everything for everyone—or they isolate and stay to themselves. As you embark on this journey of self-discovery and growth, wouldn't it be nice to share the road with fellow travelers? People you can laugh with, cry with, encourage and support? Perhaps you have discovered a specific talent or skill you have that would help others. Becoming part of a community of like-minded people can involve joining a running club, volunteering at the zoo, or writing a blog, it all depends on what feels comfortable to you. Alfred Adler said that the key to psychological health is having what he called "social interest." Instead of trying to figure everything out alone or being consumed by your own problems, a community provides mutual caring, giving, encouragement, and a sense of belonging. Feeling alone or being lonely is one of the most prevalent contributors to neurosis, depression, anxiety, and a host of other ailments that keep people from growing and feeling content. When you think about finding a community or group to participate in, think about what you have to offer as well as what it has to offer you. It should feel mutually beneficial.

Before we look at community options you might consider, let's recap some of what you've learned about yourself through this process:

Enneagram Type: _____

Focus of Life Pie: _____

Conflict/Confrontation Style: _____

Values:

Summarize what you've learned about yourself during the course of this workbook:

_____

_____

_____

_____

_____

_____

_____

_____

_____

_____

_____

Where are some places (groups, organizations, or classes) you could participate in that would help you get the support and encouragement you need to reach your goals and to make changes in your life? List 5 ideas:

1.
_____

2.
_____

3.
_____

4.
_____

5.
_____

Where are some places that could use your particular gifts and talents? List 5 ideas:

1.
_____

2.
_____

3.
_____

4.
_____

5.
_____

Pick one place from each group that you would be willing to contact this week for more information:

1.
_____

2.
_____

We've reached the end of this workbook. I want to personally thank you for having the courage to learn about covert narcissism and investigate how it may have affected your life as a child and as an adult. I know it hasn't been easy, but hopefully you have gained insight and awareness of the dynamics that have shaped your life, and are ready to begin to the next part of your journey. There are therapists who specialize in treating adult children of narcissists, and are even willing to do phone consultations if you aren't in their area. If you're already working with a psychologist or counselor, maybe bring this workbook in to them and see if it's something you could incorporate into your therapy. I do list resources in the back of the book that will help you delve into this discussion in more detail, so please don't stop here! Keep learning, keep growing, and start living your own life—on your own terms. Good luck to you!

"The world is so empty if one thinks only of mountains, rivers & cities; but to know someone who thinks & feels with us, & who, though distant, is close to us in spirit, this makes the earth for us an inhabited garden."
—*Johann Wolfgang von Goethe*

References:

Adult Children of Alcoholics World Service Organization, I. (n.d.). The laundry list. Retrieved from http://www.adultchildren.org/lit/Laundry_List.php

Ashby, H., Duke, E, & Lee, R. (1979). A narcissistic personality disorder MMPI scale. *Paper presented at the 87th Annual Convention of the American Psychological Association, New York, NY.*

American Psychiatric Association. (2013). *Diagnostic and statistical manual of mental disorders* (5th ed.). Arlington: American Psychiatric Association

Ames, D., Rose, P., & Anderson, C. (2006). The npi-16 as a short measure of narcissism. *The journal of research in personality*, 40, 440-450. Retrieved from http://www.columbia.edu/~da358/npi16/npi16_jrp.pdf

Angeli, E., Wagner, J., Lawrick, E., Moore, K., Anderson, M., Soderlund, L., Brizee, A., & Keck, R. (n.d.). Retrieved from http://owl.english.purdue.edu/owl/resource/560/14/

Ansbacher, H., & Ansbacher, R. (1956). *The individual psychology of alfred adler.* New York: Harper & Row.

Berger, L., (1982). Crime and punishment: A psychoanalytic reading. *California Institute of Technology.*

Bierhoff, H., Herner, M., Neumann, E., & Rohmann, E. (2012). Grandiose and vulnerable narcissism: Self-construal, attachment, and love in romantic relationships. *European Psychologist*, *17*(4), 279-290.

Bradshaw, J. (1988). *Healing the shame that binds you.* Deerfield Beach: Health Communications

Campbell, W., & Miller, J. (2010). The case for using research on trait narcissism as a building block for understanding narcissistic personality disorder. *Personality Disorders: Theory, Research, And Treatment*, *1*(3), 180-191. doi:10.1037/a0018229

Cheek, J., & Wink, P. (1990). Shyness and narcissism: Are they related? *Unpublished manuscript.*

Davis, R., & Millon, T. (1996). Disorders of personality: DSM-IV and beyond (2nd ed.). New York: John Wiley & Sons.

Dickinson, K., & Pincus, A. (2003). Interpersonal analysis of grandiose and vulnerable narcissism. *Journal of Personality Disorders, 17*(3), 188-207.

Emmons, R. A. (1987). Narcissism: Theory and measurement. Journal of Personality and Social Psychology, 52, 11-17.

Golomb, E. (1997). *Trapped in the mirror.* New York: Harper Paperbacks.

Graham, J., (1987). The MMPI handbook. *New York: Oxford University Press.*

Hall, C., & Raskin, R., (1979) A narcissistic personality inventory. *Psychological Reports, 45, 590).*

Hall, C., & Raskin, R. (1981). The narcissistic personality inventory: Alternative from reliability and further evidence of construct validity. *Journal of Personality Assessment*, 45, 159-162.

Hammer, E., Giordano, P., & Lindley, N. (1999). Codependency predictors and psychometric issues. *Journal of Clinical Psychology*, 55(1), 59-64.

Hendin, H. & Cheek, J. (1997). Assessing hypersensitive narcissism: A re-examination of murray's narcissism scale. *Journal of Research in Personality,* 31, 588-599.

Holahan, C. K., & Spence, J. T. (1980). Desirable and undesirable masculine and feminine traits in counselling clients and unselected students. *Journal of Consulting and Clinical Psychology*, 48, 300-302.

Kernberg, O. (1975). Borderline conditions and pathological narcissism. *New York: Jason Aronson.*

Luchner, A. F., Mirsalimi, H., Moser, C. J., & Jones, R. A. (2008). Maintaining boundaries in psychotherapy: Covert narcissistic personality characteristics and psychotherapists. *Psychotherapy: Theory, Research, Practice, Training, 45*(1), 1-14. doi:10.1037/0033-3204.45.1.1

Maniacci, M. (2007). His majesty the baby: Narcissism through the lens of individual psychology. *The Journal of Individual Psychology*, 63(2), 136-145.

Miller, A. (1981). *The drama of the gifted child*. New York: Basic Books, Inc.

Miller, J., & Campbell, W. (2010). The case for using research on trait narcissism as a building block for understanding narcissistic personality disorders. *Personality Disorders: Theory, Research, and Treatment, 1*(3), 180-191. doi: 10.1037/a0018229

Miller, J. D., Widiger, T. A., & Campbell, W. (2010). Narcissistic personality disorder and the DSM-V. *Journal Of Abnormal Psychology, 119*(4), 640-649. doi:10.1037/a0019529

Neuman, G. (n.d.). Adult children of alcoholics. Retrieved from http://legacy.coppin.edu/ccsd/counseling/campaigns/acoa.pdf

Peck, S. (1983). *People of the lie*. New York: Simon & Schuster.

Pincus, A. L., Ansell, E. B., Pimentel, C. A., Cain, N. M., Wright, A. C., & Levy, K. N. (2009). Initial construction and validation of the Pathological Narcissism Inventory. *Psychological Assessment, 21*(3), 365-379. doi:10.1037/a0016530

Pine, C. J. (n.d.). Retrieved from http://www.apa.org/pi/oema/resources/policy/provider-guidelines.aspx

Pistole, M. (1995). Adult attachment style and narcissistic vulnerability. *Psychoanalytic Psychology, 12*(1), 115-126. doi:10.1037/h0079603

Pressman, S., & Pressman, R. (1994). *The narcissistic family: Diagnosis and treatment*. New York, NY: Josey-Bass.

Riso, D. and Hudson, R. (2010). RHETI, The QUEST-TAS, the IVQ (Instincts Questionnaire).

http://www.EnneagramInstitute.com

Raskin, R., & Terry, H. (1998). A principal-components analysis of the narcissistic personality inventory and further evidence of its construct validity. *Journal of Personality and Social Psychology, 54,* 890-902.

Saragovi, C., Aube, J., Koestner, R., & Zuroff, D. (2002). Traits, motives, and depressive styles as reflections of agency and communion. Personality and Social Psychology Bulletin, 28, 563-577.

Schoenleber, M., Sadeh, N., & Verona, E. (2011). Parallel syndromes: Two dimensions of narcissism and the facets of psychopathic personality in criminally involved individuals. *Personality Disorders: Theory, Research, And Treatment, 2*(2), 113-127. doi:10.1037/a0021870

Scribner, C. (2001). Rosenhan revisited. *Professional Psychology: Research and Practice, 32*(2), 215-216. doi:10.1037/0735-7028.32.2.215

Sedikides, C., Rudich, E. A., Gregg, A. P., Kumashiro, M., & Rusbult, C. (2004). Are Normal Narcissists Psychologically Healthy?: Self-Esteem Matters. *Journal Of Personality And Social Psychology, 87*(3), 400-416. doi:10.1037/0022-3514.87.3.400

Smolewska, K., & Dion, K. (2005). Narcissism and adult attachment: A multivariate approach. *Self and identity, 4,* 59-68.

Solomon, R. S. (1982). Validity of the MMPI narcissistic personality disorder scale. *Psychological Reports,* 50, 463-466.

Sperry, L. (2003). *Handbook of diagnosis and treatment of dsm-iv personality disorders.* New York: Brunner-Routledge.

Stein, H. (n.d.). *The feeling of inferiority and the striving for recognition.* Retrieved from http://www.adlerian.us/tp-8.htm

Stein, H. (1997). *Stages of classical adlerian psychotherapy.* Retrieved from http://www.adlerian.us/stages2.htm

Stein, H., & Edwards, M. (n.d.). *Classical adlerian theory and practice.* Retrieved from http://www.adlerian.us/theoprac.htm

Watson, P. J., Taylor, D., & Morris, R. J. (1987). Narcissism, sex roles, and self-functioning. Sex Roles, 16, 335-349.

Wilson, S., & Durbin, C. (2012). Parental personality disorder symptoms are associated with dysfunctional parent-child interactions during early childhood: A multilevel modeling analysis. *Personality Disorders: Theory, Research, And Treatment, 3*(1), 55-65. doi:10.1037/a0024245

Wink, P. (1991). Two faces of narcissism. *Journal Of Personality And Social Psychology, 61*(4), 590-597. doi:10.1037/0022-3514.61.4.590

Made in the USA
Coppell, TX
25 January 2021

48803792R00049